The
Presidents
of the
United States

The Marshall Cavendish illustrated history of

The
Presidents
of the
United States

PUBLIC LIBRARY
MAR 1 2 1991
SOUTH BEND, INDIANA

Written by
Ruth Oakley

Illustrated by
Steve Lucas and Tim Woodcock-Jones

MARSHALL CAVENDISH
New York · London · Toronto · Sydney

Library Edition Published 1990

© Marshall Cavendish Limited 1990
© DPM Services Limited 1990

Published by Marshall Cavendish Corporation
147, West Merrick Road
Freeport
Long Island
N.Y. 11520

Series created by Graham Beehag Book Design
Designed by Graham Beehag
Produced by DPM Services Limited

All rights reserved. No part of this book may be reproduced or utilized in any form or by any means electronic or mechanical including photocopying, recording, or by any information storage and retrieval system, without permission from the copyright holders.

Library of Congress Cataloging-in-Publication Data

Oakley, Ruth.
   The Marshall Cavendish illustrated history of presidents of the United States / by Ruth Oakley
     p. cm.
   Includes indexes.
   Summary: Places each American preesident in a historical context and discusses his life, with an emphasis on his political activity and presidential term.
   ISBN 1-85435-144-3 (set)
   1. Presidents – United States – Biography – Juvenile literature. 2. United States – Politics and government – Juvenile literature.
[1. Presidents.] I. Title.
E176.8.025 1990
973'.0992 – dc20   89-17283
[B]   CIP
[920]   AC

Printed and bound in the United States of America by Lake Book Manufacturing Inc.

REF j923.173 Oa4p v.2   RBF
Oakley, Ruth.
The Presidents of the
 United States

CONTENTS

Introduction

During the twenty-eight years between 1817 and 1845, there were six Presidents of the United States. They lived through a period in their country's history when political parties were becoming more organized and more powerful. By the time Van Buren was elected, it was the parties who decided on the candidates and promoted them to the voters in campaign rallies and processions.

Nevertheless, once a man was elected president, he could use the powers of the office according to his beliefs, opinions and temperament. Both Andrew Jackson and John Tyler were prepared to dismiss their cabinets and push through their policies.

The United States was growing in size and power as more and more states applied to join the union. This strengthened America's position with respect to foreign powers and enabled her to publish and

The Monroe Doctrine asserted that the Americas had the right to determine their own destiny free from European interference.

maintain the Monroe Doctrine. At the same time, it weakened the hold of the southern states, particularly Virginia, over the main political offices. Until Andrew Jackson's election, all the Presidents, except John Adams and his son John Quincy Adams, had come from wealthy and influential Virginia plantation families.

It also made the question of slavery a potential problem. Southern landowners needed slaves to grow the cotton on which the southern economy depended. Slaves also gave them political power. A slave could not vote, but counted as three-fifths of a person for voting rights, and his owner voted for him. Some politicians wanted to see slavery abolished completely; others did not want it extended to any new states. Although compromises were reached during the period, the question remained a threat to future unity.

Southern plantation owners depended on slave labor to harvest their cotton.

7

JAMES MONROE
(1758-1831)

Fifth President: 1817-1825

James Monroe

"The Era of Good Feelings"

Family background and early life

James Monroe, like Washington, was born in Westmoreland County, Virginia. He was the second child of Spencer Monroe, a farmer and circuit judge of Scottish descent, and Elizabeth Jones Monroe, whose ancestors had come from Wales. He had three brothers and a sister.

He attended William and Mary College, the second oldest in America, but left before completing his studies to volunteer as a soldier in the American Revolution. He was wounded at the Battle of Trenton, but rose to the rank of Lt. Colonel and was well regarded by George Washington. He studied law under Thomas Jefferson, who remained a good friend and wise adviser to the younger man.

In 1786, Monroe married the beautiful seventeen-year-old Elizabeth Kortwright. She suffered from ill health in later life. As First Lady, she took a less active part in Washington social life than her predecessor, Dolley Madison, although she had been very popular in France when Monroe was a diplomat there.

The couple raised two daughters and also had a son who died in infancy.

The capital of the Republic of Liberia in west Africa is named Monrovia in honor of James Monroe. He helped to set up the state in 1822 as a home for freed, repatriated slaves.

Political experience

Monroe was a member of the Continental Congress from 1783 to 1786 and a Senator from 1790 to 1794. He opposed the Constitution in 1788, fearful that too much power was being given to the central government. Once it was passed with the first ten amendments, however, he became its defender.

He was sent abroad on several diplomatic missions, generally unsuccessful. He went to France on Washington's behalf from 1794 to 1796 at the end of the French Revolution. He was criticized for being too friendly to the revolutionary government. He returned to France during Jefferson's presidency to help negotiate the Louisiana Purchase with Napoleon, although most of the work had already been done. Jefferson also sent him to England from 1803 to 1807, but Monroe was unsuccessful in negotiating a treaty favorable to the U.S. concerning the impressment of American seamen and financial compensation for attacks on American shipping and cargoes.

He was governor of his home state from 1799 to 1802, and again in 1811. In Madison's cabinet, he was Secretary of State from 1811 to 1817 and Secretary of

The First Seminole War (1816-18) resulted in the Transcontinental Treaty of 1821. Spain ceded all her lands east of the Mississippi and all rights to the Oregon country to the United States for five million dollars. The money was to be paid to American citizens for damage to American commerce done by Spain in the European war.

War from 1814 to 1815, following the capture of the capital of Washington.

Monroe's presidency

His experience in public affairs and his close friendship with Madison and Jefferson made him the obvious Republican choice for presidential candidate in 1816, and he was elected with little opposition. The Federalists did not put up a candidate, because the differences between the Federalist and the Republican parties had become of little account. Monroe supported a tariff, a national bank and internal improvements, such as the building of roads and canals, at the expense of the national government.

Another reason for the lessening of party arguments was the end of the War of 1812 with Great Britain. The United States was becoming recognized as an independent and important nation by the great powers of Europe.

Monroe began his presidency with a tour of New England. He continued the policy of reconciliation between the parties and between different sections of the community in his choice of cabinet. John Quincy Adams of Massachusetts was Secretary of State and John C. Calhoun of South Carolina was Secretary of War.

Despite these efforts, clashes of interest between different parts of the country began to make themselves felt after 1819.

The expense and disruption of trade caused by the War of 1812 caused an economic depression in 1819. Also in that year, Missouri asked to join the Union, but wished to be allowed to keep slaves.

Slavery had been a source of argument between

James Monroe is the first President of whom a photograph exists. His home "Oak Hill" was designed by Thomas Jefferson and built by James Hoban, who also built the White House.

Negroes were transported from Africa in appalling conditions. Many did not survive the journey.

northern and southern states since the beginning of the union. The numbers of slaves had begun to diminish until Eli Whitney invented the cotton gin in the 1790s. This device had made it very profitable to raise cotton with slave labor. In Monroe's presidency, there were eleven states which allowed slavery and eleven which did not. Because the constitution counted a slave as three-fifths of a free man for the purposes of taxation and representation in Congress, the southern states would lose twenty Congressmen if slavery were abolished, since the freed slaves would not be allowed to vote.

Henry Clay helped to avoid civil war, at least for the moment, by a series of compromises. Maine was admitted as a "free" state, that is one where slavery was not allowed, in 1820. Missouri was admitted as a "slave" state in the next year. This compromise

Early attempts at photography required the subject to remain still for several minutes and the picture often gradually faded away when exposed to the light, Monroe posed for his picture to be taken in the White House.

maintained the balance between "free" and "slave" states. A law was passed that no more "slave" states would be allowed in the Louisiana Purchase north and west of the southern boundary of Missouri.

The second term

Monroe was re-elected in 1820 with the loss of only one vote. In 1823, he published what came to be known as the Monroe Doctrine. Because Spain was involved in wars with Napoleon, her Central and South American colonies had been seizing their independence. The United States had recognized

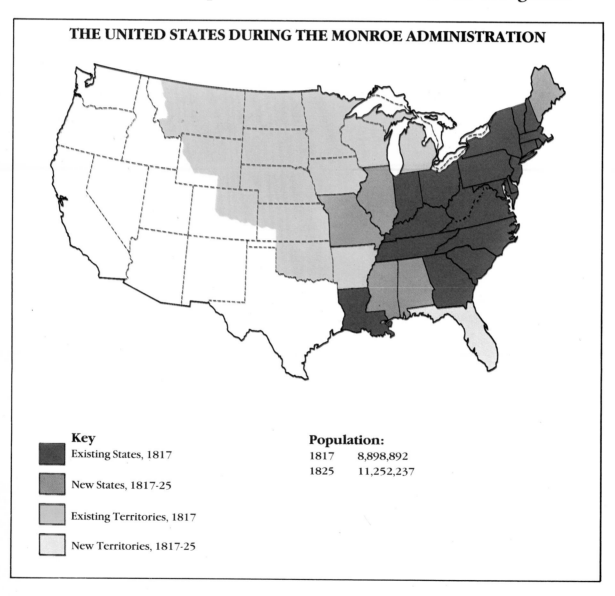

THE UNITED STATES DURING THE MONROE ADMINISTRATION

Key
Existing States, 1817

New States, 1817-25

Existing Territories, 1817

New Territories, 1817-25

Population:
1817   8,898,892
1825   11,252,237

In the Rush-Bagot Agreement of 1817, Great Britain and the United States agreed to reduce the number of armed vessels which they each had on the Great Lakes.

some of them. Russia, Prussia and Austria had united to form the Holy Alliance, with the aim of retaining the powers of their monarchies, and were prepared to intervene on Spain's behalf. Russia was also extending its influence down the west coast of North America. George Canning, the British Foreign Secretary, urged Monroe to ally with Great Britain to resist further European expansion on the American continent.

Monroe refused. He regarded Britain just as much a threat to U.S. independence as the other European powers. Monroe's statement asserted that the United States would regard any attempt on Europe's behalf "to extend their system to any part of this hemisphere as dangerous to our peace and safety." The whole of North, Central and South America were to be regarded as independent and not "as subjects for future colonization by any European powers."

The U.S. would not interfere with the existing colonies of European powers: "in the wars of the European powers in matters relating to themselves, we have never taken any part, nor does it comport with our policy so to do."

Retirement

During his retirement at Oak Hill, Monroe was short of money and was forced to ask Congress to repay the expenses which he had incurred while in office. He moved to New York City to live with his daughter and died there on July 4, 1831. Like Jefferson and Adams, he died on an anniversary of the Declaration of Independence.

Of the first five Presidents, four were Virginians.

BIOGRAPHY BOX

James Monroe

Birthplace	Monroe's Creek, Virginia
Date of birth	April 28, 1758
Education	College of William and Mary
Profession	Lawyer
Presidential term	March 4, 1817 to March 4, 1825
Party	Democratic-Republican
Place of death	New York, New York
Date of death	July 4, 1831
Place of burial	Richmond, Virginia

Monroe was the first
to live in the rebuilt
White House after
the original had
been burned down
by the British.

JOHN QUINCY ADAMS
(1767-1848)

Sixth President: 1825-1829

John Quincy Adams.

Early life

John Quincy Adams was the eldest of the five children of Abigail Smith Adams and John Adams, the second President of the United States. He was born at Braintree (now Quincy), Massachusetts, in 1767. His father had been very active in public life at a time of great change for the new United States of America. Because of this, John Quincy Adams had many experiences in his youth which broadened his outlook and were of advantage to him in his political career.

As an eight year old, he watched the Battle of Bunker Hill from a hill above the family farm. Three years later, when his father was sent on a diplomatic mission to France to negotiate an alliance between the French and the Americans, John Quincy accompanied him and was educated in Paris. John Adams then moved to Holland to negotiate a loan for the United States, and John Quincy attended the University of Leyden. He spoke French, Dutch and German fluently.

A career diplomat

His first post was as secretary to the American ambassador in Russia at the age of fourteen. On his

John Quincy Adams wrote of himself in his diary, "I am a man of reserved, cold, austere, and forbidding manners."
It is true that he had no popular appeal and few friends. For this reason, his great service to his country has gone largely unrecognized, although John F. Kennedy devoted a whole chapter to him in his Pulitzer prize-winning book, "Profiles of Courage."

return to America, he graduated from Harvard College and went on to study law. George Washington sent him to the Hague from 1794 to 1796. In his father's presidency, John Quincy was sent as Minister to Prussia from 1797 to 1801. On his return, he was elected first to his State Senate and then to the U.S. Senate as a member of the Federalist party. He did not, however, always follow the party line. This made him unpopular with other members of his party, and he was forced to resign.

From 1809 to 1814 in Madison's term of office, he was sent to Russia. He was one of the five American commissioners to negotiate the Treaty of Ghent which ended the War of 1812 between England and the United States. He then became minister to the Court of St. James in London from 1815 to 1817, following in his father's footsteps.

Marriage and family

During a visit to England, John Quincy met Louisa Johnson, the London-born daughter of the U.S. consul in London and his English wife. John and Louisa were married in 1797 in London. Louisa traveled around the world with him on his diplomatic assignments and was used to the ways of European courts. She was less at ease at first on the family farm and in Boston society when the Adamses were in New England.

They had homes in Quincy, Boston and Washington. In Washington, she had a reputation as an outstanding hostess who provided good music for her guests.

John Quincy Adams was an amateur botanist and established a botanical garden in Washington. He planted hundreds of trees in the White House grounds. His wife spun silk from the silkworms in the mulberry trees which he grew.

Louisa had periods of poor health and depression, but generally their fifty years of marriage were happy. They had three sons, and a daughter who died in infancy in Russia.

Secretary of State

John Quincy Adams was appointed as Secretary of State in Monroe's cabinet in 1817. His success in this very powerful and influential position made him a strong future Presidential candidate.

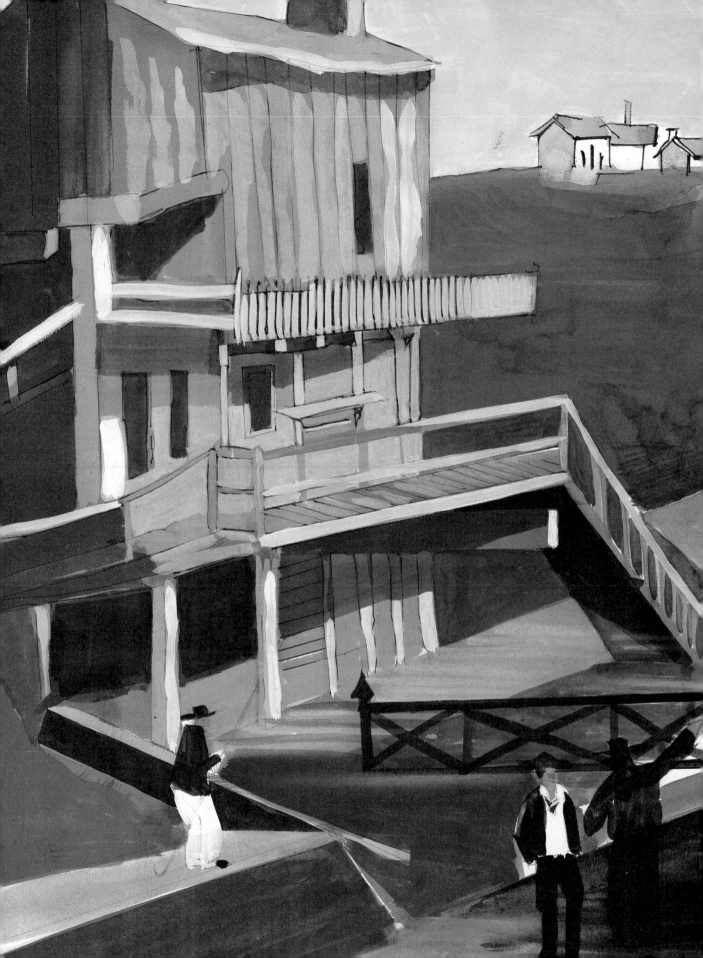

The building of the
Erie Canal opened
up routes for
improved trade and
transportation.

The Rush-Bagot Agreement (1817) with Great Britain set limits to the numbers of armed ships on the Great Lakes. Agreement was also reached between the two countries regarding the boundary between the U.S. and Canada. There was to be joint occupancy of Oregon for ten years, and the northern boundary of the Louisiana Purchase was set at the forty-ninth parallel. Spain agreed, in the terms of the Adams-Onis Treaty of 1819, that the U.S. should acquire East and West Florida and should have claims in the northwest. Quincy Adams also played a major role in the formulation of the Monroe Doctrine in 1823.

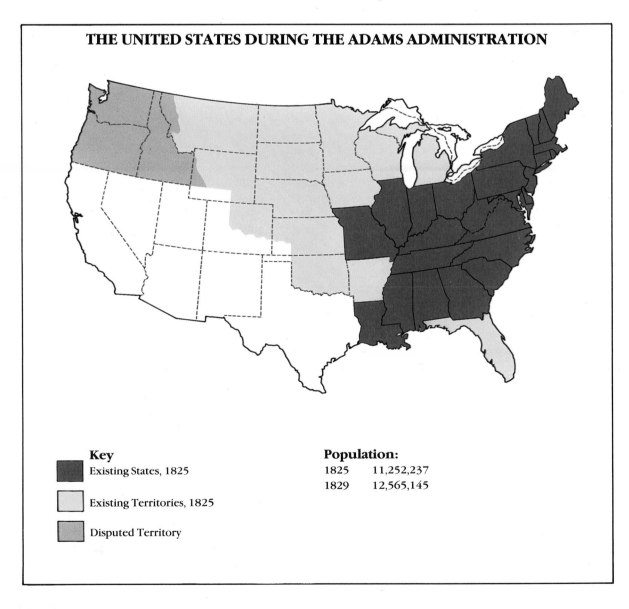

THE UNITED STATES DURING THE ADAMS ADMINISTRATION

Key
Existing States, 1825

Existing Territories, 1825

Disputed Territory

Population:
1825   11,252,237
1829   12,565,145

He worked very hard as President and had little leisure time. He liked to play billiards and to swim nude in the Potomac, which shocked some members of Washington society.

The Presidency

There were four candidates in the election of 1842: John Quincy Adams; Andrew Jackson, under whose command the American forces had won the Battle of New Orleans at the end of the War of 1812; Henry Clay and John C. Calhoun. Andrew Jackson got the most votes in the popular poll, but because there were four candidates, it was not enough to give him an overall majority. Because Henry Clay supported Adams in the deciding vote in the House of Representatives, Adams became President, with John C. Calhoun as Vice-President.

Adams faced strong opposition from Jackson's supporters during his term of office, especially as he appointed Henry Clay as Secretary of State. He had no party following of his own, and as the parties began to regain their strength and influence, Adams found it very difficult to carry out his policies. He was more tolerant toward the Indians and slaves than most people thought desirable. He raised the tariff, which was an unpopular move, and made mistakes in his foreign policy with Britain and Latin America.

In 1828, Andrew Jackson was elected President with the support of a strong party in Congress. The election campaign had been so bitter that Adams refused to attend Jackson's inaugural ceremony.

Later life

Quincy Adams continued to be active in politics, independent of party affiliations. He was a member of the House of Representatives from 1831 to 1848, where he was an outspoken opponent of slavery.

It was largely due to Adams' far-sightedness and his Congressional influence that the buildings of the

Quincy Adams
enjoyed swimming
in the Potomac.

Smithsonian Institution stand along the Mall in Washington today. This "world's greatest museum" houses scientific, artistic and historical collections.

The money to found "an establishment for the increase and diffusion of knowledge among men" was left in 1829 in the will of James Smithson, an Englishman who had never even visited America. Congress debated for ten years whether it had the right to accept the gift under the terms of the Constitution. Quincy Adams led the fight for approval.

John Quincy Adams had a stroke in the House in February, 1848, at the age of eighty and died two days later in the Speaker's room in the Capitol. He is buried in Quincy with his parents and his wife.

The Smithsonian Institution in Washington.

BIOGRAPHY BOX

John Quincy Adams

Birthplace	Braintree (now Quincy), Massachusetts
Date of birth	July 11, 1767
Education	Harvard
Profession	Lawyer
Presidential term	March 4, 1825 to March 4, 1829
Party	National Republican
Place of death	Washington, D.C.
Date of death	February 23, 1848
Place of burial	Braintree (now Quincy), Massachusetts

ANDREW JACKSON
(1767-1845)

Seventh President: 1829-1837

Andrew Jackson

"Jackson and Reform"

Childhood and early life

Andrew Jackson's childhood was very different from that of John Quincy Adams. Jackson lived in a log cabin in the Carolinas. His parents, who were poor Irish immigrants, and his two brothers were all dead by the time Andrew was fourteen.

He fought against the British Redcoats at the Battle of Hanging Rock when he was only thirteen. His dislike of the British was intensified when, as a prisoner at the age of fourteen, he was scarred for life by a slash on the cheek from the saber of a British officer whose shoes Jackson refused to shine.

He became a lawyer and attorney general in the Territorial Western District of North Carolina, then a wilderness inhabited mainly by Indians. The rule of law there needed the help of a pair of strong fists. When the Territory became the state of Tennessee in 1796, Jackson helped to write its constitution and was its first representative in Congress. He was a senator for a short time, but resigned because he felt out of place.

He became a judge in Tennessee and was a Major General in the state militia.

Jackson's nickname "Old Hickory" referred to his powers of endurance. It was first applied at the Battle of Horseshoe Bend, when he fought against the Creek Indians. He was suffering from pistol wounds inflicted in a tavern brawl and had to be lifted onto his horse. The doctors had recommended that his arm should be amputated, but he refused.

Marriage and home

He married Rachel Robards in 1791 when he was twenty-four. They both believed that Rachel had earlier been divorced by her husband. In fact, Captain Robards had only obtained permission to file for divorce. After some scandal, the couple were remarried quietly in 1794. They were very happy together, and Rachel was a kind and respected hostess at their home The Hermitage, a large house and plantation worked with slave labor, near Nashville. Jackson made his fortune by speculating in land, some of which was used instead of money by his clients to pay his legal fees. He also dealt in slaves. Although he was a hard master, he had a humane side, which he demonstrated when he traced and brought together on his estate the entire family of one of his slaves, at a cost of $1,800.00.

The Jacksons had no children of their own, but in 1809, they adopted a nephew and named him Andrew Jackson, Jr. They also brought up other nephews, including Andrew Jackson Donelson, who married his cousin Emily, one of Rachel's favorite nieces.

When Rachel died shortly before Jackson's inauguration, Emily acted as her uncle's hostess.

He wore a miniature of his wife every day and kept it by his bed at night. He fought at least two duels to avenge insults against her.

Andrew Jackson was scarred for life by a British officer, for refusing to polish his boots.

A successful soldier

His military successes made Andrew Jackson a hero among the American people and later assured him of the presidency. In the War of 1812 against Great Britain, Jackson proved himself to be a very able army

Jackson won a great victory against the British at the Battle of New Orleans.

officer. He defeated the Creek Indians at the Battle of Horseshoe Bend, Alabama, in 1814. He was appointed Major General and put in charge of the southern campaign. His victory against the British at New Orleans in 1815 was his greatest popular

A twenty dollar bill with Jackson's portrait.

achievement. His success continued during the First Seminole War (1817-18) and the conquest of Florida. He was a determined and courageous officer who was popular with his men despite being a strict disciplinarian.

A time of change

America was changing from an agricultural society dominated by large landowners in the south, to one in which industry, manufacture, foreign trade and expansion in the west played an increasingly important part. A growing number of men had the right to vote. By 1824, all white adult males had the vote except in Rhode Island, Virginia and Louisiana.

It was no longer just the two main parties – the Federalists and the Democratic Republicans – who had power. Many groups were determined to make their influence felt. Improved transport and more newspapers enabled them to make their views known to a wide audience. During Jackson's presidency, the Whig party was formed.

The people's choice

In the election of 1824, Jackson won the most votes, but did not get an overall majority. John Quincy Adams, with the help of Henry Clay, who had gained the least number of popular votes, was chosen by the House of Representatives. As far as ordinary people were concerned, Jackson was a martyr and they had been cheated out of the president they had chosen. With so much popular support in the country, Jackson's election in 1828 was almost inevitable. A bitterly fought campaign led to personal attacks on all sides, which may have been a factor in his wife's death. Jackson was inaugurated in the midst of much noisy public jubilation, which scandalized conventional Washington society.

A strong president

Although the outline of the president's powers were

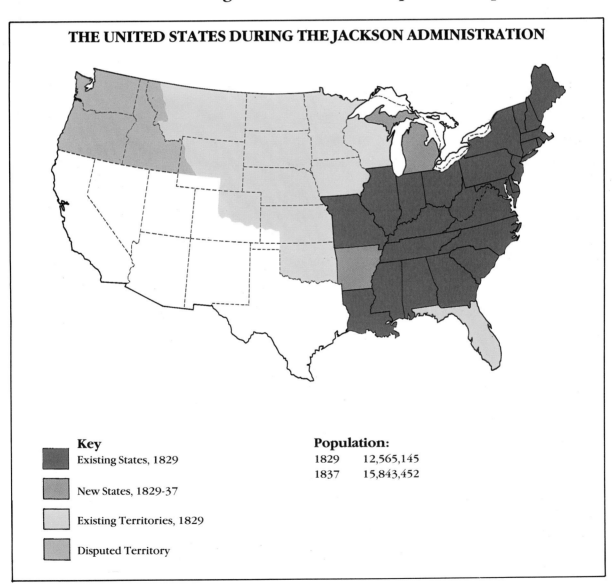

THE UNITED STATES DURING THE JACKSON ADMINISTRATION

Key
Existing States, 1829

New States, 1829-37

Existing Territories, 1829

Disputed Territory

Population:
1829   12,565,145
1837   15,843,452

> He was the first President to ride on a train, the first to keep racehorses in the White House grounds and the first against whom there was an assassination attempt.

laid down by the Constitution, Jackson was the first to combine them to assert his authority and independence. His official cabinet was composed of men with little influence, and he depended far more on a group of personal advisers. In 1831, he disbanded his first cabinet because there had been so much gossip and argument about the wife of Jackson's friend and Secretary of War, John Henry Eaton.

Although his campaign slogan had been "Jackson and Reform," one of Jackson's first acts was to remove a great number of officials and replace them with his own supporters. This, "the spoils system," had good and bad points. It can be an incentive for officials to work well for the people who elect them, but it can lead to corruption, with officials doing favors for individuals, which are not in the interest of the general population. Also, frequent changes in each post weeded out inefficiency, but it could also waste individual expertise.

The national bank

In 1832, Jackson was re-elected with a large majority over Henry Clay. One of his first problems was the Bank of the United States. Jackson did not trust paper money and suspected the Bank of using its power against him. Jackson used his right as President to veto the re-issue of the Bank's charter. In 1833, he ordered government deposits to be transferred to various state banks. This led to a struggle between banks, which caused a financial crisis as people ceased to trust the value of paper money and wanted to change it to gold or silver. Jackson refused to budge, and eventually the National Bank was destroyed.

Nullification

Vice-President John C. Calhoun was one of Jackson's chief opponents over the question of a state's right to "nullify" a federal law. This meant that a state could decide that a law passed by the government had no power in that state. In particular, the southern states objected to high tariffs which protected the manufacturing industries of the north. Jackson believed passionately that a strong union of states was essential for America to survive as a nation. He took a very firm line, threatening military intervention and said he would hang anyone who refused to pay their

Andrew Jackson was "a man of the people."

Jackson was saved from assassination due to the failure of a pistol. Although he was then sixty-eight years old he pursued his assailant and attacked him with his cane.

Black Hawk, chief of the Sauk and the Fox, refused to humble himself before Jackson when taken to Washington after being defeated in the Battle of Bad Axe.

At the Battle of New Orleans, American casualties were thirteen killed, thirty-nine wounded and nineteen missing. The British lost 291 killed, 1262 wounded and 484 missing.

customs duties. Henry Clay worked out a "Compromise Tariff" which overcame the immediate problem, but again the difference in views between North and South remained.

The Indians and foreign policy

Jackson was very harsh in his treatment of the Indians, against the advice of the Chief Justice, John Marshall. On Jackson's orders the Five Civilized Nations were moved to present-day Oklahoma. The Seminoles were moved by the Second Seminole War of 1835-1842. In foreign affairs, Jackson failed to purchase Texas and California from Mexico. He supported the Texas Revolution of 1835. He reached financial agreements with France, Great Britain, Siam and Muscat.

Later life

Jackson did not seek re-election in 1836 as his health was failing. His chosen successor, Martin Van Buren, became the eighth President. Jackson continued to send advice from The Hermitage until his death there in 1845.

BIOGRAPHY BOX

Andrew Jackson

Birthplace	Waxhaw settlement, South Carolina
Date of birth	March 15, 1767
Education	Self-educated
Profession	Lawyer and soldier
Presidential term	March 4, 1829 to March 4, 1837
Party	Democrat
Place of death	Hermitage, Tennessee
Date of death	The June 8, 1845
Place of burial	The Hermitage, Tennessee

MARTIN VAN BUREN
(1782-1862)

Eighth President: 1837-1841

"The Little Magician"

Family background

Martin Van Buren was the first American president who was not of British descent. His ancestors were Dutch, who settled in the Hudson River Valley in about 1633. He was also the first President who was born a citizen of the United States, and the first to have played no part in the American Revolution against British rule. He was born at the time of the birth of the new United States and lived long enough to see it torn apart by the outbreak of civil war.

He was born in 1782 in Kinderhook, Columbia County, New York, the third of five children. He was educated locally until he was fourteen, when he was apprenticed to a local attorney. He set up a successful legal practice in his hometown, where he married his cousin and childhood sweetheart, Hannah Hoes. They had five sons, one of whom died in infancy.

In 1816, the family moved to Albany, the state capital, where Hannah ran a busy, contented and sociable household. This happiness did not last long, however. Hannah died in 1819, aged only thirty-five, probably from tuberculosis, and Van Buren never remarried, although he was an eligible widower.

Van Buren was nicknamed "Old Kinderhook" from his birthplace and used the abbreviation "O.K." as a campaign slogan. This is probably the derivation of the term.

Personality

Martin Van Buren was a charming and likeable man who was also cautious, crafty and very ambitious. He skillfully manipulated people and events to his own advantage. He used his power to reward his supporters with lucrative and influential government posts and to remove those who opposed him. He was very good at being on the winning side and was generally careful not to commit himself too strongly to any position or cause. However, as President, he did pursue what he knew to be a very unpopular policy over a serious financial depression. He was prepared to use his influence to gain power, but he was never dishonest over money, although to do so would have been easy for him.

Powerful friends

It was due very much to the influence of Andrew Jackson, the seventh President, that Van Buren was elected in 1836. Van Buren had been a loyal supporter of Jackson for many years and had used his political skills to mastermind Jackson's victory in 1828. He had been a state senator and had built up a powerful political machine in New York for the Democratic Republican party. He was elected to the U.S. Senate from 1821-8. During that time, he had opposed John Quincy Adams and supported Jackson.

Van Buren was Governor of New York for a few

John Randolph of Roanoke wrote of Van Buren, "He rowed to his object with muffled oars," a comment on Van Buren's craftiness.

months and then entered Jackson's cabinet as Secretary of State from 1829 to 1831. He visited England briefly; then he ran for Vice-President following the resignation of John C. Calhoun. He was elected, and in 1835, he was unanimously elected as the Democratic candidate for the presidency.

Routes by which the pioneers explored the West.

The financial depression

Van Buren inherited serious financial problems from Andrew Jackson. Many people were pushing west to settle new lands. Speculators bought land with paper money at a fixed price from the government, which

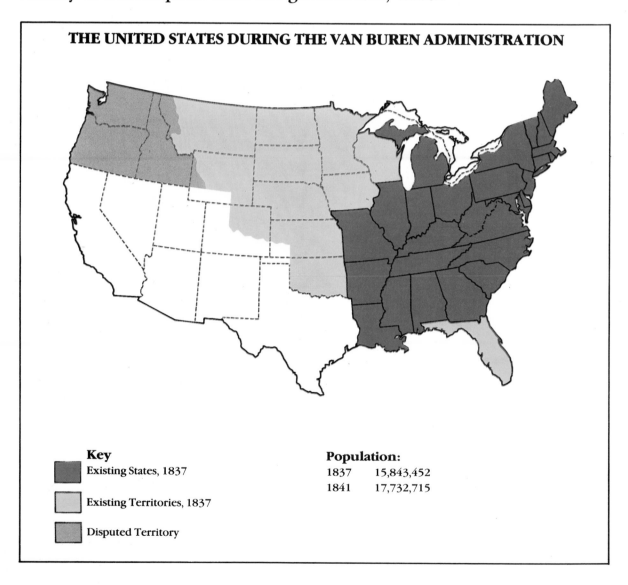

THE UNITED STATES DURING THE VAN BUREN ADMINISTRATION

Key

Existing States, 1837

Existing Territories, 1837

Disputed Territory

Population:

1837	15,843,452
1841	17,732,715

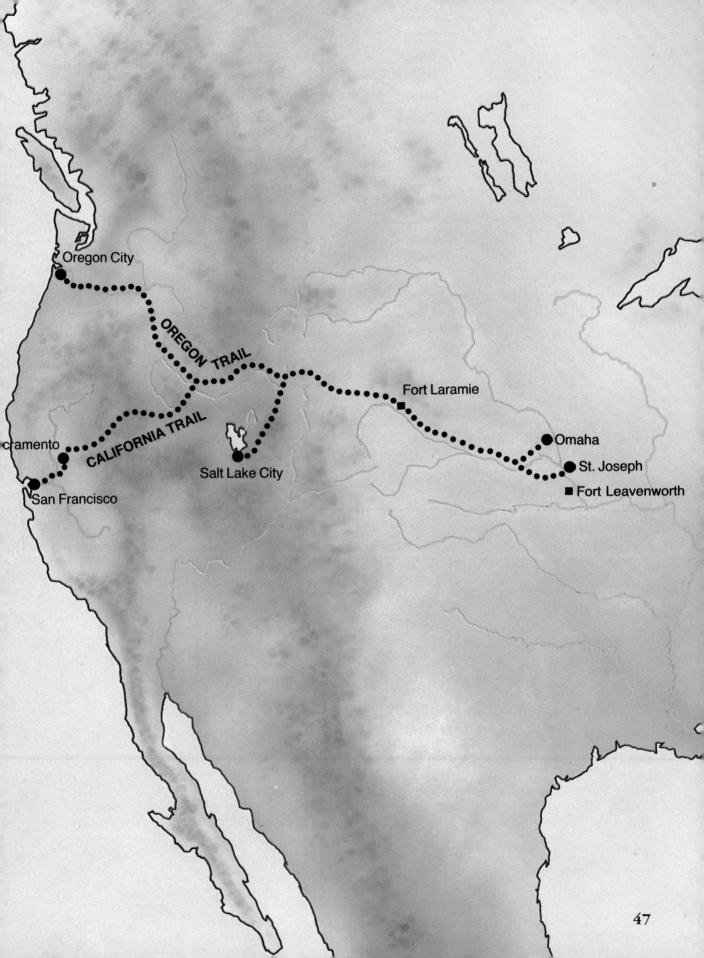

Oregon City

 OREGON TRAIL

Fort Laramie

CALIFORNIA TRAIL

cramento

Omaha

Salt Lake City

St. Joseph

San Francisco

Fort Leavenworth

47

they resold to settlers at much higher prices. Jackson ruled that the speculators had to pay in gold or silver, and he refused to re-charter the United States Bank. When people lost confidence that banks would honor their notes and began to demand to be paid in gold or silver, a financial panic resulted.

The price of land dropped. People lost money and suffered a great deal of hardship. Van Buren refused to let the federal government intervene, believing it was best to let prices find their own level. He was probably correct, but it appeared to the electors that he did not care about the people's problems. His stand on this issue was one of the main reasons that he was not re-elected.

A pioneer family stop for rest beside their covered wagon.

Making a home in Indian country.

Later life

When he left office, Van Buren went to live on his estate near Kinderhook, but he was still active politically. He made two further unsuccessful attempts at nomination in 1844 and 1848. He died in 1862 during the Civil War, fully supporting Lincoln's policies to preserve the Union and to limit slavery.

BIOGRAPHY BOX

Martin Van Buren

Birthplace	Kinderhook, New York
Date of birth	December 5, 1782
Education	Public schools
Profession	Lawyer
Presidential term	March 4, 1837 to March 4, 1841
Party	Democratic
Place of death	Kinderhook, New York
Date of death	July 24, 1862
Place of burial	Kinderhook, New York

WILLIAM HENRY HARRISON
(1773-1841)

Ninth President: 1841

Family background and early life

William Henry Harrison was elected as the candidate of the newly formed Whig Party. He was represented as being a plain man of the people, a Western pioneer and soldier. In fact, he was born in 1773 to a wealthy Virginia family of British descent with royal connections. His father, Benjamin Harrison, had been a signatory to the Declaration of Independence.

William Henry studied medicine at Richmond and moved to Philadelphia to continue his studies when his father died in 1791. Harrison decided to join the army and make his living as a soldier. He was appointed to the First Regiment of the United States Infantry. At the Battle of Fallen Timbers against the Indians in 1794, he served as aide-de-camp to General "Mad Anthony" Wayne.

In 1795, Harrison married Anna Tuthill Symmes, against her father's wishes. They had six sons and four daughters during their life together.

Indiana territory

A campaign pamphlet for "Old Tip."

Harrison's political progress began in 1798 with his appointment as Secretary of the Northwest Territory. The following year he was elected as Territorial

HARRISON'S HUMANITY IN WAR.

THE COUNCIL OF VINCENNES,
On the memorable 12th of August, 1810,
Where Tecumseh appeared with three hundred warriors, and attempting an insurrection, was subdued by the presence of mind and courage of Harrison.

HARRISON SAVING THE LIFE OF A NEGRO.

ILLUSTRATED INCIDENTS
IN THE LIFE OF
GEN. WILLIAM HENRY HARRISON.

HARRISON'S HUMANITY IN WAR.

"Go!" exclaimed the generous Harrison, "go and take the town. But let an account of murdered innocence be opened in the records of heaven against our enemies alone. The American soldier will follow the example of his government; and the sword of the one will not be raised against the fallen and the helpless, nor the gold of the other be paid for the scalps of a massacred enemy!"

HARRISON'S ADDRESS TO BOLIVAR.

"In this enlightened age, the mere hero of the field, and the successful leader of armies, may, for the moment, attract attention, but it will be such as is bestowed upon the passing meteor, whose blaze is no longer remembered, when it is no longer seen. To be esteemed eminently great, it is necessary to be eminently good. The qualities of the hero and the general must be devoted to the advantage of mankind, before he will be permitted to assume the title of their benefactor; and the station which he will hold in their regard and affections, will depend, not upon the number and the splendor of his victories, but upon the results and the use he may make of the influence he acquires from them."

HARRISON'S TREATMENT OF AN OLD FELLOW SOLDIER.

While General Harrison was seated with a few friends at dinner, an old soldier entered to pay his respects to his Commander-in-chief. Harrison, instantly recognizing him and shaking him cordially by the hand, turned to his guests, saying, "Gentlemen, let me introduce an old friend and companion in arms; he will take a seat at the table." The guests, rose and received the soldier. He was then seated next to the General, and they all passed the evening in social conversation. When the party retired, Harrison presented the soldier with a new coat, and the veteran, overwhelmed with gratitude, bade adieu to the Log Cabin and its hospitable owner.

HARRISON PREFERRING ANOTHER MAN'S SON TO HIS OWN.

While General Harrison was Governor of Indiana, he entertained an intention of applying for a position for his son at West Point. There was only a single vacancy, and he would certainly have obtained the desired appointment. In the meanwhile, a neighboring farmer applied to Harrison to exert his influence for him, as he also desired such a place for his boy. The noble-hearted chief, ever ready to do more for others than for himself promptly complied with the man's request, and used his influence to obtain the situation which was wanted.

HARRISON'S CARE FOR HIS SOLDIERS.

The cut represents one of the characteristic traits of Harrison, in which he is personally binding up the wounds of a soldier.

THE EAGLE OF FORT MEIGS.

The General remarked that he thanked his friends of Crawford County for the present they were so obliging as to send him. Their request should be attended to; he would keep the Eagle until he could see the country restored to its liberty, either by this or any other administration; until men could go to the polls and exercise the elective franchise without fear or compulsion, by office-holders or others; until the people of this country could be free and independent, and the legislation of the country should be left to be done by the Legislature, and not the Executive. Then, and not till then, would he give the bird its freedom, that it might wing its way to its native air, and perch itself upon the tree of liberty, and be indeed the true ensign of our country's standard."

HARRISON SAVING THE LIFE OF A NEGRO.

Frequent attempts had been made to assassinate Harrison, and before the action of Tippecanoe, a negro was arrested, who was lurking near the Governor's marquee with the intention of killing him in his sleep. At the time of the action, this fellow was a prisoner in the camp. After the battle, a drum-head court martial was called to try the negro who was convicted of deserting to the enemy, under circumstances from which it was conjectured that he had returned to the camp for the purpose of assassinating the Governor. He was sentenced to suffer death. The sentence was approved, and he was to be executed in one hour; but Harrison pardoned him.

THE COUNCIL OF VINCENNES.

The cut represents General Harrison at the memorable council of Vincennes, subduing the haughty and rebellious spirit of Tecumseh. An instance of presence of mind which saved the people of the town from a most horrible scene of bloodshed.

HARRISON GIVING HIS HORSE TO A METHODIST MINISTER.

Many years since, while the hero of the Thames was on a hot summer evening, at the porch of his humble "Log-Cabin," he was asked for shelter and a meal, by a minister of the Methodist Episcopal persuasion. After a plain and substantial supper, they retired to rest, the good old soldier thankful to a munificent Providence, that he was enabled to administer to the wants of a fellow creature, and the worthy minister of Christ, invoking the blessing of Heaven upon the head of his kind benefactor. Morning came, and the minister prepared to depart. He was in the act of taking leave, when he was informed that his horse had died during the night. But taking his saddle-bags on his arm, he rose to depart with thanks for the kindness of his entertainer. The old General did not attempt to prevent him. The guest reached the door, and to his astonishment, found one of the General's horses accoutred with his own saddle and bridle, in waiting for him. He returned and remonstrated, stating his inability to pay for it, and that in all probability he should never again visit that section of the country. But the General was inexorable, and reminding the astonished Divine, that "he who giveth to the poor lendeth to the Lord," sent him on his way, his heart overflowing with gratitude, and his prayers directed to Heaven for blessings on the venerable Hero.

HARRISON GIVING AWAY HIS ONLY BLANKET.

During the pursuit of Proctor, all Harrison's baggage was carried in a valise, and his bed was a single blanket fastened over his saddle. This last he gave to Colonel Evans, a wounded British officer.

HARRISON'S SELF-DENIAL.

It often happened to Harrison and to his troops, while engaged in the terrible warfare which his genius so happily terminated, to suffer great privations. Frequently their provisions were so scanty that there was not enough to divide among the men. On such occasions, Harrison would not take a morsel while there was one common soldier to be provided, and the cut represents him declining the proffered food, like a generous-hearted, self-denying patriot.

HARRISON CHARGING IN BATTLE, AT THE THAMES.

One of his aids just before had entreated him not expose his person, which was so valuable to his country; but determined to share the danger of his brave troops, Harrison could not be prevailed on to regard his own safety, but putting spurs to his horse he broke away from his friends, and was instantly, sword in hand in the thickest of the battle.

HARRISON'S ADDRESS TO BOLIVAR.

HARRISON'S TREATMENT OF AN OLD FELLOW SOLDIER.

HARRISON PREFERRING ANOTHER MAN'S SON TO HIS OWN.

HARRISON GIVING HIS HORSE TO A METHODIST MINISTER.

HARRISON GIVING AWAY HIS ONLY BLANKET.

HARRISON'S SELF-DENIAL.

DELIVERING THE EAGLE.

HARRISON'S CARE FOR HIS SOLDIERS.

"Majestic monarch of the cloud,   To hear the tempest trumping loud   When strive the warriors of the storm,   Child of the sun! to thee 'tis given
Who rear'st aloft thy regal form,   And see the lightning lances driven,   And rolls the thunder-drum of heaven,   To guard the banner of the free."

HARRISON CHARGING IN BATTLE, AT THE THAMES.

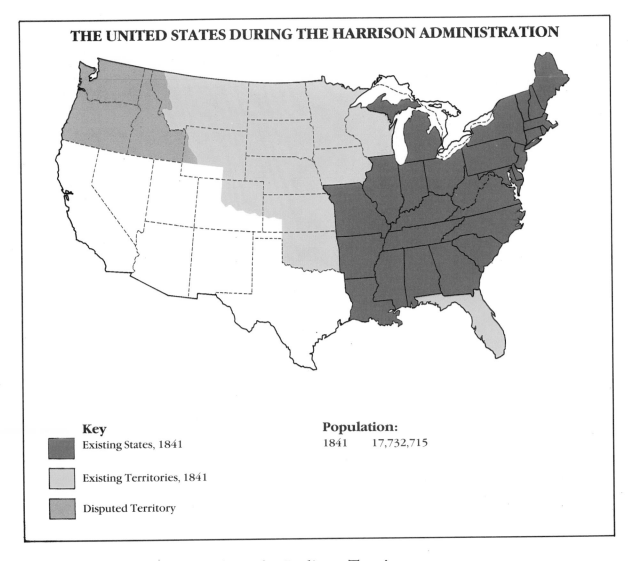

THE UNITED STATES DURING THE HARRISON ADMINISTRATION

Key

Existing States, 1841

Existing Territories, 1841

Disputed Territory

Population:

1841   17,732,715

Delegate to Congress. When the Indiana Territory was formed in 1800, Harrison became its Governor and served for nearly thirteen years. He continued the policy of persuading the Indians to relinquish their tribal lands so the country could be opened up to white settlers. Chiefs were often persuaded by providing them with whisky and getting them to sign treaties when they were drunk.

Tecumseh and Tippecanoe

Tecumseh was an Indian of unusual foresight, leadership and ability. He persuaded a large number of braves from different tribes to ally together, live peaceably and industriously and resist the selling of

A campaign handkerchief given to one of Harrison's supporters.

Harrison called his house at Vincennes, Indiana, "Grouseland," because he was very fond of shooting and fishing.

William H. Harrison was the last President to be born a British subject. He was the first to die in office and the first to die in the White House. He served the shortest term.

any more Indian land. Tecumseh argued that the land belonged to the tribe as a whole and the chiefs had no right to sell it. His brother, a medicine man known as The Prophet, assisted him by telling the Indians that the Great Spirit approved of Tecumseh's ideas. Also, the British supported Tecumseh against the Americans.

While Tecumseh was gone on a visit to southern tribes, Harrison marched against the Indian village of Tippecanoe. After a skirmish outside the village,

The Battle of Tippecanoe.

Harrison marched in and destroyed it, discrediting The Prophet, who had told the Indians they would win easily.

This was regarded as a great victory for Harrison. More success followed. At the Battle of the Thames in 1813 against British and Indian fighters, Harrison commanded the victorious U.S. forces. Tecumseh was killed and with him died hopes of an Indian confederacy.

"Tippecanoe and Tyler too"

Harrison's nickname, "Old Tip," came from the Battle of Tippecanoe. It was part of a political campaign by the leaders of the Whigs to portray him as a trusty, down-to-earth soldier and pioneer compared to Van Buren, the smooth, sophisticated politician.

Harrison's previous political experience was as a Congressman from 1816 to 1819 and a Senator from 1825 to 1828. He was chosen as the presidential candidate because he had not made enemies by taking a strong line on any particular policy. The party machine built him up and staged publicity stunts, such as displaying miniature log cabins in their processions and serving cider at their rallies. These measures increased public interest in the election, and the turnout of voters was much larger than in the past.

It seems ironic that after all this excitement, Harrison only lived for thirty-one days after his inauguration. He died from pleurisy and pneumonia in April, 1841.

BIOGRAPHY BOX

William Henry Harrison

Birthplace	Berkeley, Virginia
Date of birth	February 9, 1773
Education	Hampden-Sydney
Profession	Soldier
Presidential term	March 4, 1841 to April 4, 1841
Party	Whig
Place of death	Washington, D.C.
Date of death	April 4, 1841
Place of burial	North Bend, Ohio

JOHN TYLER
(1790-1862)

Tenth President: 1841-1845

John Tyler

"Honest John"

John Tyler was the first Vice-President to become President as a result of a president's death in office. After William Henry Harrison's death only a month after his inauguration, there was some dispute as to whether it was constitutional for the Vice-President to take up the office of President without an election. Tyler settled the matter by sending Congress a note signed "John Tyler, President." He showed a similarly forceful attitude to powerful members of his cabinet, such as Henry Clay and Daniel Webster, when they tried to usurp his authority.

Family life and marriage

John Tyler was born in 1790 near Greenway, Virginia, where his father was Governor. He was the sixth of eight children, with five sisters and two brothers. After attending the College of William and Mary at Williamsburg, he became an exceptionally successful lawyer.

He married Letitia Christian, the daughter of a Virginia planter, in 1813. They had five daughters and two sons. Letitia was crippled by a paralytic stroke two years before Tyler became president. From a second-floor room in the White House, she played an

> **Tyler called his home "Sherwood Forest," after the legendary Robin Hood's territory because he felt himself to be a political outlaw.**

important role in family life, but her daughter-in-law, Priscilla Cooper Tyler, took over the social duties of the administration and acted as hostess. Letitia died in 1842, the first President's wife to die in the White House. Tyler remarried in 1844. His bride, Julia

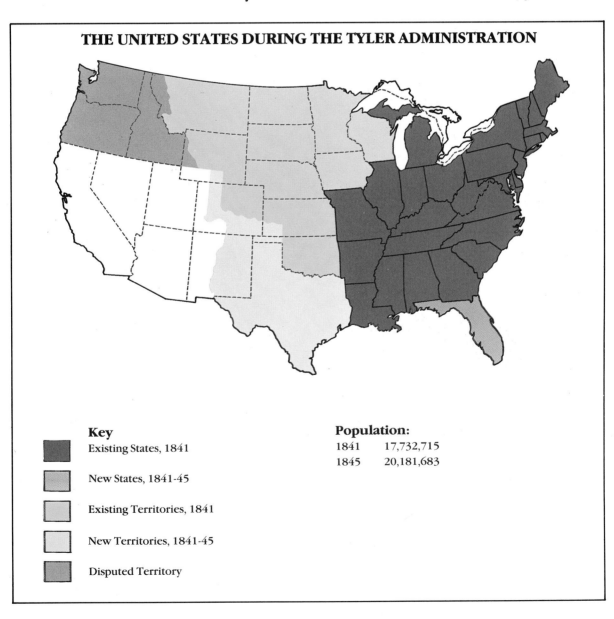

THE UNITED STATES DURING THE TYLER ADMINISTRATION

Key

- Existing States, 1841
- New States, 1841-45
- Existing Territories, 1841
- New Territories, 1841-45
- Disputed Territory

Population:

| 1841 | 17,732,715 |
| 1845 | 20,181,683 |

Tradition has it that John Tyler was playing marbles on his farm in Virginia when the news of President Harrison's death reached him. He rode the 230 miles from Williamsburg to Washington on horseback in twenty-one hours.

Gardiner, was a well-known society belle from a wealthy New York family. Despite the thirty-year difference in their ages, they were a devoted couple. Julia enjoyed her position as First Lady, but was content to retire to Tyler's home at Sherwood Forest, Virginia, when his term of office was over. They had five sons and two daughters.

Tyler's political experience

His political life began as a member of the Virginia House of Delegates from 1811-1816 and again from 1823-1825. He was Governor of Virginia from 1825-1826. He served in both houses of Congress: in the House of Representatives from 1816-1821, and as a Senator from 1827-1836.

He was first a Democratic Republican and then a Whig. He supported the rights of individual states and opposed a national bank, high tariffs and internal improvements. Well-liked and well-respected, he became Vice-President to Harrison in 1840.

His Presidency

Although Tyler had been elected with Whig support,

Tyler narrowly escaped death in 1844 when he was on board the USS Princeton to see the firing of the "Peacemaker," the world's largest naval gun. It exploded, killing the father of Tyler's second wife, the Secretary of State and the Secretary of the Navy.

58

The famous painter of Indians, George Catlin, produced this dignified portrait of Osceola, leader of the Seminole Indians.

he was not in favor of all their policies. When he vetoed a bill for a new Bank of the United States, his entire cabinet, except Daniel Webster, resigned, and Tyler was expelled from the party.

Despite not having the support of a party, Tyler managed to achieve some notable successes. He ended the Second Seminole War, settled a boundary dispute with Great Britain by the Webster-Ashburton treaty, reformed the navy and refused to use the spoils system.

The most important, however, was the incorporation of Texas into the United States from Mexico. This annexation was finally accepted by Congress just before he left office, despite fears that pro-slavery policy in Texas might upset the balance between the northern and southern states.

John Tyler was the first President against whom an impeachment attempt was made. To impeach a President means to accuse him of being unworthy of the office and to remove him from it. The reason in Tyler's case was his continual blocking of legislation passed by Congress by his use of the presidential veto. This resolution was defeated in the House of Representatives by 127 votes to 83.

Later life

After the election of James K. Polk in 1845, Tyler retired from public life. He had not run as a presidential candidate since he had no party support.

In 1861, he chaired a conference in Washington which failed to avert civil war. When war did break out, he was a member of the provisional Confederate Congress. He died in 1862 in Richmond, Virginia.

BIOGRAPHY BOX

John Tyler

Birthplace	Greenway, Virginia
Date of birth	March 29, 1790
Education	College of William and Mary
Profession	Lawyer
Presidential term	April 4, 1841 to March 4, 1845
Party	Whig
Place of death	Charles City, Virginia
Date of death	January 18, 1862
Place of burial	Richmond, Virginia

Davy Crockett died at the Battle of the Alamo against Mexico.

GLOSSARY

aide-de-camp — an officer acting as confidential assistant to a senior officer

Attorney General — chief legal officer of a state

cabinet — a small group of government officials who decide what the government should do

confederation — a union, or joining together, of states

constitution — the laws and agreements which give a government its powers

depression — a time when people lose confidence in the business dealings of a country. Trade slumps, causing large losses and great financial hardship

emancipation — setting free, especially from slavery or unjust laws

federal — relating to the central government of a group of states who have agreed to unite, as distinct from the governments of the individual states

internal improvements — the building of roads, canals, railroads and other public works carried out by the federal government

militia — a military force, usually made up of ordinary citizens in an emergency to reinforce the regular army

nullification — the policy that each state has the right, if necessary, to ignore a federal law

speculators — people who invest in a business which is likely to be risky, but which will bring large rewards if successful

spoils system — the custom of rewarding a president's supporters with government posts and removing those who did not aid him

tariff — a law imposing customs duties on exports and imports. In the United States in the nineteenth century, the tariff was used to protect home industry from foreign competition

veto — the president's right to reject a law which Congress voted to enact

INDEX

Numbers in *italics* refer to illustrations.

Adams, John 7, 15, 18
Adams, John Quincy 7, 10, 18-29, 30, 37
Adams-Onis Treaty 24
Alabama 34
Albany 44

Bank of the United States 38, 48, 59
Battle of Bad Axe *42*
Battle of Bunker Hill 18
Battle of Fallen Timbers 50
Battle of Hanging Rock 30
Battle of Horseshoe Bend 31, 34
Battle of New Orleans 25, *34*, 35, 38
Battle of the Thames 55
Battle of Tippecanoe *54*
Black Hawk *42*
Boston 19
Braintree 18
Buren, Martin Van 6, 43, 44-9, 55

Calhoun, John C. 10, 25, 43, 46
California 43
Canada 24
Canning, George 15
Carolinas, the 30
Christian, Letitia 56-7
Civil War 49, 61

Clay, Henry 11, 25, 37, 38, 43, 56
Continental Congress 9
cotton 7, 11
Crockett, Davy (David) 61

Declaration of Independence 15, 50
Democratic Republican party 37, 45, 46, 58
Donelson, Emily 31

Eaton, John Henry 38
England 9, 19, 46
Erie Canal *22-3*

Fallen Timbers, Battle of 50
Federalist party 10, 19, 37
First Seminole War 9, 35
Florida 24, 35
France 8, 9, 18, 43
French Revolution 9

Gardiner, Julia 57-8
Ghent, Treaty of 19
Great Britain 10, 15, 19, 24, 34, 35, 43, 54-5, 59
Great Lakes 24

Harrison, Benjamin 50
Harrison, William Henry 50-5, 56, 58
Harvard College 19
Hoban, James 10
Hoes, Hannah 44

Holland 18, 19
Holy Alliance 15
Horseshoe Bend, Battle of 31, 34
House of Representatives 25, 37, 58, 60

impeachment 60
impressment 9
Indiana Territory 52, 53
Indians 25, 30, 31, 34, 42-3, 50, 52-5
internal improvements 10, 58

Jackson, Andrew 6, 7, 25, 30-43, 45, 46
Jefferson, Thomas 8, 9, 10, 15
Johnson, Louisa 19-21

Kennedy, John F. 19
Kortwright, Eliza 8

Lincoln, Abraham 49
Louisiana 36
Louisiana Purchase 9, 14, 24

Madison, Dolley 8
Madison, James 9, 10, 19
Maine 11
Marshall, John 43
Massachusetts 18
Mexico 43, 59
Mississippi, the 9